WHERE GOD MET ME

WHERE GOD MET ME

REDEEMED FROM A PATH OF FAILURE

JOANNA BECK

Unless otherwise indicated, all scripture quotations in this book are from the *King James Version* of the Bible. Take note that the name satan and related names are not capitalized. I choose not to acknowledge him, even to the point of violating grammatical rules.

Visit author's website at www.bushelandabeck.com

INTRODUCTION

I am here to tell you, you do not have to live a broken life. You can live the full life Jesus died to give you. When all you see is darkness think about this: Even though you do not feel God's presence, it is still there. Even though you do not see His hand, it is still moving. Even when you do not hear His voice, He is still speaking, even in the silence. Even when you feel abandoned and alone, still His love is there. And even when He seems hopelessly far away from you, He is still right beside you, working every detail in your life for His purposes and your redemption. And in the end, the light will break through the darkness, the good will prevail, and you will know you were never alone. He was with you all along. The pain we endure is a part of life here on earth.

When we experience pain we often question God. Do you not care God? Are you even real?Many times we create messes by bad choices we have made and when we experience the pain we then get mad that we are in the mess. That is what I had done. Divorced, depressed, and moved back in with my grandfather, I started a journey to find the real me, who I was created to be. One of my toughest choices was to no longer blame others for my situation and give God permission to heal me.

Heartbreak is real, fear is real, and the pain we feel of our heart breaking in two is real. It is said that most people would rather have a broken bone than feel heartbreak. After my divorce and custody battle my body literally ached day and night. I could not eat, I could not sleep and, I would lay in bed sobbing begging God to take the pain away.

Yet, He was silent. After years of fighting with my ex I was to what I thought was my breaking point, and then God met me in the lobby of the court house, He said: Joanna be still my child and know that I am God. After that encounter, I got intentional about my relationship with God. I was raised in a broken home. Attending church on the weekends with my grandparents, where I witnessed the wrath of men who disfellowshipped one person after another for sinning, instead of showing forgiveness and showing God as the loving Father He is. God has used every single thing I have experienced and witnessed to propel me into the purpose He has for me.

Seasons can sometimes be dark and scary but, there is always purpose for our pain. Sometimes God has to take everything away from us to show us who we are without it and who we can be in Him. The redeeming power of Jesus is amazing but, getting to the point of experiencing it can be very painful. You have to trust God in the lonely and dark times and let Him form you.

Philippians 1:6 tells us, "And I am certain that God, who began the good work within you, will continue his work until it is finally finished on the day when Christ Jesus returns."

Heartbreak, pain, and loss are all inevitable. However, it is all in how you move forward from it. Are you going to be a victim or a victor? Get better, not bitter.

What the devil meant for evil God is using for good! Right now as you read this He is turning your trials into testimonies. He wants to transform every part of your life but you have to cooperate with Him. God is a gentleman, He will not come into a place He is not welcomed. Let God heal you, every area of your life.

This is what I did, my goal was to allow God to make every broken piece within me whole. This same decision is yours and your healing is on the other side of your surrender to God. Do you want to be whole? Do you want to be healed?

"Crowds of sick people—blind, lame, or paralyzed—lay on the porches. One of the men lying there had been sick for thirty-eight years. When Jesus saw him and knew he had been ill for a long time, he asked him, "Would you like to get well?" "I can't, sir," the sick man said, "for I have no one to put me into the pool when the water bubbles up. Someone else always gets there ahead of me. " Jesus told him, "Stand up, pick up your mat, and walk!" Instantly, the man was healed! He rolled up his sleeping mat and began walking!" John 5:3,5-9.

I invite you to take a journey with me as I tell you of how God has redeemed me from a path of failure. Today I am married to an exceptional man of God. Together we share four amazing, beautiful girls and we are privileged to serve weekly in our home church in Tulsa, Oklahoma. My number one mission is to decrease hells population!

I declare over you right now that your future will be greater than your past. That this year will truly be your best year yet and that restoration is on its way in Jesus mighty name. Are you ready? Ready to believe in Gods goodness? Are you ready to see where God met me and where He is patiently waiting to meet you?

CHAPTER ONE

Whether you live a long or short life on this earth you will feel hurt and at some point you will feel stuck. Maybe it was a bad childhood or a divorce that spun you out of control.

Let me tell you until you experience the pain of divorce, you could never imagine the toll it would take on you, your children, and everyone around you. Maybe it was the blinding pain of losing a loved one or maybe you have been abused by a family member. This pain will paralyze you, and the devil will everyday have you reliving the pain and heartache. That hurt will bleed onto the people who do truly love you. These are the people that are in desperate need of a new life in Christ Jesus and the amazing news is that life is available for anyone who wants it.

I was a mess, for years I tried to be what, "I thought," everyone wanted me to be. For the people on the outside my life looked put together. I had a nice home, nice car, dressed in nice clothes, though my marriage was a roller coaster, we had more bad days then good. I lost myself, I compromised my identity to have someone love me.

My divorce wreaked me and devastated my girls, for months I questioned God as sadness took over my life. Until I finally decided I was NOT what happened to me! I was determined to get unstuck. It was a slow but steady process but, I did not give up until I experienced victory. God had always wanted to heal me, yet I was too filled with the why me and there was no room for Him.

John 4 verses 7-38 gives us the story of the woman at the well. This woman integrity was compromised. She was fearful of what others thought of her, but Jesus called her out of her mistakes and made her whole. She reached out to Him and just like today one encounter with Jesus will change your whole life and everything around you. However, I will tell you everything you do outside of God will cost you more than you could ever afford.

That is how sin is, one season will cost you a spouse, your children, your job, and anything else that means anything to you. If you continue to walk around thinking theres no hope, and if you think theres no light at the end of the tunnel, thats exactly what you will get, darkness.

I had played the victim in my own story for a long time. Although, if I had continued to play the victim, and never saw the hope or the light at the end of my tunnel you would not be reading this book today.

Are you playing victim in your story? Are you making excuses for it because of what you have been through? Because of the toxic marriage? Because you were sexually abused as a child? Are you stuck in your past? Painful experiences will brand us just like cattle if we let them.

Gen. 7:39-50 tells us of Joseph. Joseph's brother called him a dreamer but, he was so much more than that he was an interpreter of dreams. He was an honorable man. However, before anything good happened in Joseph's life he was misunderstood, falsely accused, imprisoned, and forgotten. I can identify myself with this story, I myself have been labeled, misunderstood, and accused, still God had and has a predestined future for me. I had to walk through hell on earth to get to the wholeness Jesus had for me but, that was only so I could come out on fire! Traumatic life experiences will produce side effects that will trickle down from generation to generation.

The side effects of my divorce was anger, depression, and I felt as if I had to make my marriage work for my girls. After my divorce I could not give my girls the emotional support they needed so I spoiled them with anything they asked for. Which ultimately made me feel like a double failure. Depression and sadness overwhelmed me daily. I would replay the final days and months of my failed marriage to see what I could have done differently. As memories replayed I was overtaken with shame, guilt, and anger.

You might be where I was, in the fight of your life, all you want is darkness, more sleep, and you feel most protected with the covers up over your face. You want to shut out the whole world, and you have no motivation. You are well aware your decisions have led you here but, the side effects now seem unbearable. I could not believe I was divorced, something I had sworn I would never be. I came from a broken home, my parents divorced when I was around 5 years old and my father signed over his rights shortly after. He chose drugs and alcohol over me and my siblings. The only good example I had were my grandparents, whom I compared everything to. They were childhood sweethearts and stayed together until the day my grandmother went home to be with the Lord in her 60's. Why could I not hold my marriage together like them? When I got married I had thought it was going to be forever, till death do us part.

No one in their right mind gets married and thinks oh, if this does not work, I will just find another one! No one wants a failed marriage! No one wants to be abused by a spouse, abandoned by a parent, or rejected by loved ones! This is why prayer and obedience to God is so important.

God's guidance, answers, and ways are always perfect, ours are NOT. We create these storms in our lives and then wonder why we are even in the mess. Then shake our fist at God because He is letting us deal with the consequences of our own actions. Remember, you can always pick your sin but, you can not pick your consequences. Some decisions have more serious consequences than others do, but they all produce some level of consequence. God puts it very simple when He says that "we reap what we sow" (see Galatians 6:7). When we have been hurt we make excuses for ourselves, thinking we are justified in holding grudges towards those who hurt us. We set ourselves up for failure when we blame others for our situations and then allow those difficult times to define our lives. When all along we make our own choices. We decide to enter into that relationship, to have sex before marriage, all are our decisions.

You will never avoid consequences in life, you will have to face everything at some point, because, if you do not it will destroy you. The result of bad choices can be overturned by making good choices. How you speak about your situation will also determine how long you stay in it.

The Bible tells us that life and death are in the power of the tongue and those who love it eat its fruit, see Proverbs 18:21. Your words will affect you positively or negatively that choice is yours. Look in the Bible at Numbers 13:26-34 and think of the Children of Israel. They wandered around a desert for 40 years because they chose to complain rather than praise God for delivering them from bondage and preparing something great for them.

Your words matter and words spoken over you by others matter too. I used to rage on the inside when someone would tell me "what they would do in my shoes" yet they had never been in my shoes and never experienced the pain and hurt I had. Those people who would tell me just to suck it up I wanted to break their legs and tell them to walk it off!

The things that Jesus experienced in His humanity equipped Him as a merciful high priest who could sympathize with the weaknesses and needs of all people. Sometimes we must go through things in order to fully understand the difficulties that others experience. I believe that each thing we go through helps equip us. Going through hurt helps us learn that we can endure difficulties. Hurt is not a joke, the pain everyday people feel from devastating life situations is real, and we will never know what we would do in another persons situation until it happens to us. When we are in difficult seasons it is easy to speak negativity into your life. Remember, the power you hold in your tongue, the power to cause life or death. Your life can not help but become what you have spoken. You will even surround yourself with people who feel the same way about life that you do in that season. Take a good look at your friends, they represent what your life will be and they are prophesying into your future.

Some people need to just watch you from a distance. This is not you being mean its about caring about yourself and your future! I made this mistake when I was going through my divorce. I did not want people around me that were going to tell me I was wrong for the way I felt, I wanted people who fed my anger and hatred towards my ex. Thank you Jesus for healing my heart, helping me forgive my ex husband, and put those so called friends in the bleachers so they can watch from a distance and no longer speak into my life. I decided I wanted friends that were going to pray me back to life! Think about this, if you are on your death bed do you want a friend who is going to plan your funeral or a friend that is going to pray you back to life!

I was raised in a home where disfunction was normal and I let that disfunction carry me into my future. I was never taught to love myself. I felt invaluable, rejected, and unworthy. God has done a great work in me over the years, but none of it started until I surrendered to Him and allowed Him to do it. God showed me how valuable I am to Him.

Even if the world says you are unloveable ,remember, God loved you and wrote out every day of your life before you were ever in your mothers womb. You are loved and can learn with the help from God to love yourself. People learn a lot about love from people who do not know how to love at all. Gods love goes on and on, is never-ending, and is unconditional, so why not let Him teach you about love. Break the cycle, you do not have to accept everything you are handed. If you were handed a not so glamorous childhood like me do not accept it, break that generational curse in Jesus name! I realized that God my Father had always planned for me to be here and He used my parents to get me here. He saw me. He wrote my future in His book before I took my first breath. He chose me to be His and to leave a mark on this earth.

I never felt worthy and my family had low expectations of me so they enabled my poor choices, never challenging me to be better. I never had a father that loved me and showed me an example of how a woman was to be treated. My father leaving me and my siblings at a young age left a pit of abandonment in me which caused low self esteem. Ultimately causing me to allow people to treat me poorly and talk to me with little to no respect. We hold the power to change the way we are going, the way we allow others to treat us and we are free to live abundantly because we are free to change our minds everyday.

You can say no, I will not be defined by my past and my past is not my future. My best days were not when I was in high school, no ones are if you have Jesus as your Lord and Savior. Your best days are yet to come. If you think your life here on earth is living your best days then you will be in for a big surprise when you step into eternity. Remember you have God's DNA and He determines your future.

The pain of giving the most precious part of myself to someone and them betraying it paralyzed me. I could not eat or sleep. All

I would think about was what I could have done differently. How could I have been what they wanted because I could not imagine life without that person. Bringing God into my situation was my only hope. Sometimes, fear of being alone sets in because we have a deeper rooted issue of abandonment and we stay stuck in toxic relationships that cause us more harm than good.

I got determined to constantly remind myself that God was bringing my restoration. Do not give up even if you do not see immediate changes, mine took years, yes you read that right, "years". God is always working behind the scenes!

He is your comforter and He is always there with you. I can tell you from my past experience God will use your darkest seasons to catapult you into your best days yet. To walk in true freedom, I had to renew my mind. I had to transform the old patterns of thinking. The only way to do this is to read God's word and declare the opposite of what had been spoken over my life for years. I had to replace every lie with God's truth until it became my normal way of thinking. The Bible is clear when it says, " Do not conform to the pattern of this world, but be transformed by the renewing of your mind."

When you begin to look at your problems as lessons it helps you gain control of your emotions. In the midst of a hard season we all want the pain to go away but what we really need is to learn the lesson God is teaching us.

I was a slow learner and had to learn the hard way. I got myself into situations not pre destined by God and had to then deal with the consequences. I desperately needed God to change me. Kneeling and hands lifted to heaven, crying out to God, the vail was finally lifted from my eyes and I saw clearly the attack the enemy had launched on my life. That punk devil tried to take me out from the beginning. So I had shifted my anger, I no longer hated my ex husband and everyone else who had hurt me. I hated the devil! He is the liar! He comes to kill, steal, and destroy not only us but everyone and everything we love.

One lesson I learned was without the pain I endured I would have never discovered I am a warrior, Gods warrior. What the devil meant for evil God is using for good! You might think you are too far gone, you are at rock bottom, you do not know what else there is to do. Well if you are at rock bottom let me tell you about that rock, it is Jesus. Understand this, that if there is breath in your lungs, God is NOT finished with you yet. There is hope. Your future will be so much better than your past. Praise God you are a victor and not a victim.

Paul tells us in Romans 8:31, "If God is for us, who can be against us." If you believe God is for you then act like it.

CHAPTER TWO

I have experienced intense challenges in life most of which I brought on myself but, some were specifically from the enemy.

The devil knew if I understood who I was in Christ. I would be a force to be reckoned with. I was going to help depopulate hell and boy that made satan mad. The devil is scared of a christian who grabs ahold of the power that is within them. The devil does not fight us because we are weak, he fights us because we are powerful. And, if you did not have something worth stealing the devil would never mess with you.

Remember, the same power that rose Jesus from the grave lives on the inside of you. You are strong, bold, and courageous. All of hell shook the day you were born. The devil recognizes a righteous person, a warrior, a hope dealer, a kingdom builder. That is why you feel stuck. Can you see it now? The devil is trying to drag you to hell, and he is trying hard. Are you going to let him?

Renew your mind on all the things God says about you and all the promises He has made to you. Have strong faith.

Faith like the woman who thought, "if I could only touch the hem of His robe I shall be made well." (Matthew 9:20-22).

Reach out and touch Jesus. This woman bled for twelve years but, in a moment was made well. You may feel like your storm is raging on and on, but if you reach out and touch Jesus everything will change. Maybe in a moment, maybe in a week, maybe in a year, but it will change.

God is for you, not against you. He will give you a hope and a future. Praise God for sustaining you in the stormy seasons you thought were going to take you out.

Until I surrendered to God I never had a breakthrough. I just could not get rid of the feeling of rejection and abandonment. I had to surrender my emotions, and give my feelings to God, and let Him heal them. Allowing Him to show me the plan and purpose He had for me. When I finally did experience my breakthrough it was an amazing victory.

What was once my mess is now a message. I now walk in a greater freedom more than I could have ever imagined. I am proof, your storm does NOT define your future!

All you need to do to live in this freedom is to tell God you can not do this without Him. Give Him free rein over your life and ask Him to change you. God is never ignoring you, He is silently preparing you for battle, for greatness, and for blessings.

I reached a breaking point that I had no choice but to face the issues that tormented me and held me hostage. I had let so much hurt build up, my heart was so broken, I was not a very nice person.

Are you at a breaking point? Are you tired of being upset all the time, carrying around the pain and hurt from your childhood? Are you ready to face the issues that have tormented you and held you hostage in your mind and emotions for all these years? It is time to admit you have held on to that hurt for far too long! It is time to let go. It is time to forgive, drop the extra baggage you have been carrying around and say God it is yours! Where God wants to take you, all that hurt, rejection, fear, and turmoil can not go. So leave it at the feet of Jesus.

I used to think the way people had spoken to me as a young girl did not bother me until as an adult I found myself referring to myself as those hurtful words. Think about this insecurity produces fear, worry, and anxiety, but security produces boldness and courage. It is easy to adopt an identity based on what other people say and think about you. Adopting what they speak over you will make you lose sight of who and whose you really are. Most of our unhappiness and frustration in all areas of life can be traced back to our insecurities, but thankfully we have and answer in Jesus.

Proverbs 4:23 says... "Watch over your heart with all diligence, for from it flows the springs of life." The enemy can not destroy you unless you let him! He will distract you and try his hardest to get you to focus on anything other than God. Start speaking positive over yourself and even your children reminding yourself and them you are the daughter or son of the most high

King. Focus on what God says about you.

I would not listen to my grandmother and insisted on learning the hard way. I was so blinded I honestly thought I knew what was best for me. There are two times in my life within the same year I found myself disappointing my grandmother. First, when I had to tell her I was pregnant and second, when I was getting married to that man just because I was pregnant. She begged me not to marry him, telling me everything would be ok, my home is with her and I was making a mistake. So in my rebellion, I found myself in a dysfunctional marriage. That wreaked havoc on my entire life. I often wondered how in the world did I get here, and then remembered by the choices I made.

I continually felt rejected and unprotected by some of the most important people in my life. I was in an eight year downward spiral. I tried to hold everything together for the sake of my girls, but after a while I felt as though every promise made was broken.

The devil had even convinced me I deserved all the negative things that were happening to me. So I put on that fake smile and arose day after day doing everything expected of me. No one knew the hurt and rejection I felt.

I remember sitting in my car asking God where are you!? How did I get here? My life was no where close to what I had envisioned as a little girl. Where was the happiness I expected from marriage? Where were my butterflies and white picket fences?

Out of embarrassment we often hide our struggles and difficult seasons. When we keep our pain a secret our hearts become hardened and sad instead of believing what our Heavenly Father has said about us,

"That we are fearfully and wonderfully made. I praise you because I am fearfully and wonderfully made; your works are wonderful, I know that full well." - Psalm 139:14

We put on fake smiles which are ultimately our masks and over time that pain becomes who we are, not just what has happened to us. The devil loves for us to hold onto stuff and he continually reminds us of our past in hopes he can derail us from our future. The devil can see who you are even from a young age. he knows he can not take you out so he is trying to wear you out. he wants you to lose heart, to lose faith in God. It is really a shame the devil sees more potential in us than we see in ourselves.

The enemy would love for you to hold onto bitterness, un-forgiveness, anger, and resentment that turns into hatred. It will eat away at your soul. You may have lost hope but, if you make the decision now to stay committed to God, He will take you from glory too glory. Read, study, meditate on God's Word. His Word will renew your mind, and fear will turn into faith and courage. satan has no defense against the word of God. He has no choice but to withdraw in defeat. This is why we have to stay focused. You must cooperate with God for your healing and breakthrough. Remember even when God seems silent He is still doing a mighty work. In Gods silence we can discover who we are.

We discover our strength when we go through pain and are still alive. Do not let the devil sit in your ear and remind you of all your mistakes and all you lack. Focus on what is good, pure, holy, and righteous. Take the steps in faith that God leads you to take even though you might still feel fear and insecurities, as you move forward you will begin to sense more and more freedom.

Philippians 4:8-9 tells us. "Fix your thoughts on what is true, and honorable, and right, and pure, and lovely, and admirable. Think about things that are excellent and worthy of praise. Keep putting into practice all you learned and received from me everything you heard from me and saw me doing. Then the God of peace will be with you".

All those people that have torn you down in life will watch as God builds you up. Quit blaming people, places, and things for you being where you are today. Forgive every hurt and God will right all your wrongs. He will give you double for your trouble, walk in that freedom.

Real change begins when we fully surrender to God and allow Him to transform us and our situations. You can not do it alone you need Gods help. We all have circumstances in our lives that can derail us and prevent us from moving forward if we pay excessive attention to them. Change will always requires a new direction. It means moving away from any unwise decisions, people, places, or things.

I am no stranger to change. In 2013 I felt lost and hopeless and changed my entire life. It was messy and I fought God every step of the way. I can remember yelling at God, begging Him to take the overwhelming pain and sadness I felt. There must be another way God, I pleaded. But His response never changed He wanted me to move. Within twenty-four hours of Him telling me to go my emotional state was distraught to say the least, every ounce of me was fighting God. Going meant leaving my girls behind due to our custody arrangement, leaving family and friends, and leaving ninety percent of my belongings. I could only take what I could fit in my car. Sometimes we need to get away from circumstances, we need to get unstuck.

I can relate to how Jacob felt in Genesis 32:22-32. Jacob wrestled with God and was then blessed and renamed. At the time it was painful but, looking back God was helping me break soul ties before I ever even knew what they were. Playing the victim was doing me no good and complaining never changed anything.

Our situations might be different but do you feel a hurt like this, if so then change is just what you need. Let go of the people, places, and things holding you back from your healing. Remember hurt people, hurt people. Go give yourself time and let God heal you.

Sticking around the wrong people stunts your growth and letting your painful past define your future will keep you stuck.

That is what I did, I tried stabilizing what God was trying to remove. I was so stubborn that when God dealt with me spiritually I was like the prodigal son in Luke 15:11-32. I was lost and had been found but I could not receive Gods grace, mercy, and purpose until I was willing to release that stubbornness. We are strengthened as we deal with difficulties like these, we become stronger in our faith and abilities. Thank God I had finally became honest with myself and realized my un-forgiveness had me stuck in a toxic pattern. I was so busy trying to teach other people lessons for hurting me that I was missing out on what God really had for me. God does not want us to just drop some of our baggage, He wants it ALL.

I had always looked to others to satisfy needs I had that only

God could fill. I wanted to control my life because I did not trust anyone. Today, I can tell you there is a space in your heart strictly meant for God that no friends, relationships, family, music, school, degree, or money will ever fill. Life is not meant to look how we think it should.

Philippians 4:11 tells us... "...be content regardless of your circumstances."

Allow your circumstances to educate you, not to dictate your future. Being content is not a place we can go to or a vacation we can take, it is a choice, you must choose to be content. Paul said, "invite contentment by thinking on things that are pure, just, noble, lovely, and of good report." - Philippians 4:8.

When you allow the Holy Spirit to work on you from the

inside, you become a victor instead of a victim. Being content means being a victor, even if your outside situation has not yet changed.

A victor not only wins the war but continues to slay giants.

"The righteous person may have many troubles but the Lord delivers him from them all." Psalm 34:19.

Let the Lord go before you, He will guard you and protect you in the storms. No one is perfect and everyone at some point will face a storm. Life is never fair. "We have an enemy who prowls like a lion looking for whom he may devour." (1 Peter 5:8). When you receive Jesus as you're Lord and Savior you accept His forgiveness and you know without a doubt that He is working all things together for your good. Even when you can not see Him, you trust Him. You believe in His finished work on the cross and you believe that He did it for you.

Jesus' sacrifice on the cross made salvation available to anyone who would receive it. Even if you were the only person on this earth Jesus would have done it all just for you. You are so important to Him that He would have taken all of those stripes just for you. He would have said it is finished and died just for you. Nothing you can do will make Him love you more or less. His love is unconditional. He already knew every mistake you would make even that high school pregnancy. He knew your father would not be the father you needed and that you would end up looking for love in all the wrong places. He knew about that divorce you would get.

God knew before the foundation of the world that the walls you would build around your heart would keep out your blessings. He knew you would strive for your parents approval, that you would never get. God knew all of this yet, he still loves you and validates you. He knew that I would go through all I have and write this book and you would read it one day. He saw me experience an awakening that allowed me to walk away from my past and finally experience my future. Sometimes we get lost and instead of receiving Gods grace we punish ourselves. Every season is apart of a grander story God is weaving together and He so graciously gives us a say in the outcome. You can decide right now to let go of the past and quit trying to right all the wrongs done to you. Your freedom is right in front of you.

"...It shall be done for you as you have believed..." - Matthew 8:13

By faith God created the world we live in. Many people have done seemingly impossible things by faith. Faith is leaning entirely on God in absolute trust and confidence in His power, wisdom, and goodness (see Colossians 1:4).

As my world feel apart I had to decide was I going to be pitiful and bash my ex every chance I had for the rest of my life, tearing apart my girls emotionally, or was I going to become powerful and show my girls what the transforming love of God can do. God uses people with the worst pasts to create the best futures. He will use the broken to help heal others. We have a promise from God that as we obey and serve Him, He will not only be with us Himself, but He will give His angels special charge over us.

It is so important to stop trying to impress people and start being effective for God. He will never let what you lost be the best you will ever have. Your best is yet to come if you are willing to let God do a work in you.

Looking back when I found myself getting a divorce, losing my marriage, home, car, and dignity, I had expected God to take care of me and not let me suffer. Yet everything was still about me, I thought the whole world revolved around me and my needs. I was so caught up in how hurt I felt and what I needed, I completely missed the beautiful picture God was painting.

It took me a while to grasp this and even grasp a smidge of how much He truly loved me even though I had made horrible mistakes.

After I let go of me, the fear set in of what do people think of me. I learned I could not let what people thought about me distract me from what I knew about myself. People pleasing will get you stuck living a life you never wanted because the reality is you care more about what people think than what God thinks. The fear of not being in control is one of the most prevalent fears people have. Gradually God delivered me from this fear and I was able to take my eyes off of people, things, and self and get out of acting off of my emotions. Anytime you base a decision off of what others think pride is involved.

Proverbs 16:18 tells us, "pride goes before destruction and a heavy spirit before the fall." It saddens me to see men and women bound up by their circumstances, refusing to let go of their pride and hurt in order to find freedom.

"You can do all thing through Christ, who gives you strength." - Philippians 4:13.

You have to make a choice to obey His will or yours. It is that simple. Pride is what caused me to pretend I was ok and act like I still had it all together when on the inside I was a total mess. To experience freedom you have to be honest with yourself and start to realize what you have allowed in your past is not what you want in your future. Ask yourself hard questions like.. Why is my life always full of drama? Why am I the common denominator? No one likes to take ownership, it is easier to blame others but, the truth is until you let go of all the brokenness nothing will ever change. You will spend thousands on therapists, get addicted to prescribed medications, and still find no peace! You will wear yourself out. It is just not worth it! You are so valuable to God, so much more than you could ever realize. Instead of thinking how hard it is to change switch you're thinking to how good your life will be once you are set free.

God's plan is quite different from ours. He gives us the ability to make our own decisions and He will try to guide us, but He will not force us to do the right thing. We sometimes allow ourselves to stay in repeated cycles and we find it harder and harder to change, so we accept what we do not deserve. If nothing changes you feel safe even if it means you are living in hell. You are allowing life to pass you by. That is not God's Will for your life. If you do not know what His will is read His word. God spoke the universe into existence and breathed life into us. Do you not think He wants the best for you?

I have yet to meet one person that has not experienced pain. Everyone has lost something or someone. How you deal with the pain is what is important. Are you an overcomer or a dweller? I myself have done both. When I dwelled, I existed just to exist, I never noticed the beauty in things like flowers, or the sky at sunset and sunrise. Our lives are like a canvas and God is the artist attempting to paint a perfect picture. Imagine if an artist was painting a picture and the canvas refused to stay still.

The project would be a mess; and this is often what happens to our lives. I refuse to let my life be a mess. When I decided to overcome I got bold with the devil, throat punched him and sent him and every demon he sent to take me out back to where they belong, in hell! Then once I found courage I could look at the sky and its like watching the heavens open and shine Gods glory everyday.

You do not have to accept everything that is thrown at you. Learn to expect the unexpected this is simply accepting that we cannot control all of life and then trusting God will enable us to deal with things as they come. Even if you do not know what to do in your situation right now, you can still walk in forgiveness and repent of the choices you have made that lead you to this place of pain. As long as we are on this earth we will encounter storms. The good news is every storm runs out of rain. Storms come in seasons. They may only last one season or a few but, no storm is a life sentence. You cannot avoid them and you cannot control them. We must come face to face with our issues and admit these strongholds will not go away by themselves. You can however control your responses. God has promised to never let more come on us then we can bear and to also always provide a way out (see 1 Corinthians 10:13).

The devil laughs when you ask him to please leave you alone, use your authority, get bold with him, tell him enough is enough! Whether you are in a storm right now or you can see one coming, this is the perfect time to ask God into your situation so He can guide you and begin to break every generational curse off of you.

Generational curses are real! It may have run in your family but, this is where it runs out! When you receive Jesus into your heart, He lives on the inside of you. That means the same power that rose Jesus from the grave lives in you and will set you free from bondage! You can not be healed from pain you ignore and suppress. You have to deal with whatever has devastated you, hiding from it and numbing it will not help you sleep at night. If you want to be free be honest with yourself and God.

CHAPTER THREE

We are told time after time in the Bible to watch what we speak for the tongue holds the power of life or death. And if you realized how powerful your thoughts are, you would never think a negative thought again. Do not copy the behavior and customs of this world, but let God transform you into a new person by changing the way you think.

"Then you will learn to know God's will for you, which is good and pleasing and perfect." - Romans 12:2

Death is saying I will never win, I will never find a better job, I will never get a promotion, No one will ever love me, No one wants to marry me. Recognize the strength God has given you, renounce the negative things you have spoken over your life and start to confess everything good into your life.

Hebrews 13:5 tells us, "He will never leave us nor forsake us."

You are never alone God is with you always. Do not allow your past hurts to navigate your relationship with Jesus Christ. Your relationship with Jesus will never ever compare to earthly relationships. We are all broken vessels and the devil wants us to fail but, failure is not defeat unless you quit!

Leave negativity behind you. Stop allowing people to highjack your faith and stop allowing them to stop you from stepping into your healing. You can not heal what you are unwilling to reveal. Especially if shame is involved. If you allow it, shame will over rule you, it will keep you bound to your pain and your past. However, when you finally realize your freedom in Jesus Christ you will not allow shame to keep you from revealing your past.

For many years I did not like to talk about my first marriage and share that my daughters did not live with me, especially to strangers. I wanted to pretend like it never happened, but it did and it is part of my past. Revealing that part of my life was part of my healing. I finally realized in order for me to help others be set free from strongholds, I first needed to break mine. What happens to us is not only about us, it is about all those people out in this world who need someone to speak up and say look, look how my life was, look what I have been through and look where I am now!

It is time for you to have a discussion with God about who you are becoming, what your true identity is, and who He has called you to be. It does not matter who you were in the past, what matters is who you are after you encounter the overwhelming healing love of God. That one decision changes everything. My hurt sparked a change in how I show the love of Jesus to not only myself but others who cross my path as well.

The choice I made to release all un- forgiveness, bitterness, and anger created the platform I have today. No one in my life could ever give me the satisfaction God did when I allowed Him to heal me.

You also have a call from God on your life to do great things. We have been chosen by God, picked out as His own in Christ before the foundation of the world (see Ephesians 1:4). The enemy will do everything in his power to distract and destroy you before you step into your purpose. No matter how bad you are hurting, I urge you to pray! Pour your heart out to God and do not worry about sounding eloquent. Tell Him how you feel and be patient as He works in your life. I admit that it is difficult to be patient when you are hurting, but God will comfort you as you remain in faith. It is up to you to move from where you are right now to where you are destined to be. God loves to take His children from glory too glory. The life I lost will never compare to the life I have now. He has and continues to bless me beyond what I could ever ask or dream. My life is full of exciting new experiences.

Many of the storms in my life were created by my choices. Some happened when I was placed in detrimental places by others actions and I had to survive the chaos that surrounded my life at that time. Gods divine protection kept me from dangers seen and unseen. Based on what I know He had protected me from, I can not imagine what the unseen was. God's hand was and still is on my life. His hand has always been on your life as well.

There is a reason why people hurt others, it is because they are hurt and broken on the inside. Once I received healing, I was able to see others through a different lens. The lens I now look through is one of love and forgiveness, which has helped me comprehend how the people who have hurt me in my life have been victims of abuse and negativity from people in their lives. I understand now that their actions towards me were not against me personally. It is a generational pattern that stops with me. I put a stop to the cycle of control, manipulation, anger, fear, emotional breakdown and gossip. I think that anyone who has experienced rejection and then recovers from it is actually stronger than someone who has never experienced those feelings at all. Being knocked down in life and getting back up helps us build a resolve that is vital for victory.

And always remember hurt people hurt people, healed people heal people.

When I allowed God to heal my heart and take away my pain, the marriage I used to pray God would erase from my memory became a marriage I was thankful for because it gave me two of my greatest gifts, my girls. Because of what God has taught me I will always be thankful to Him for letting me walk through a very difficult season and for bringing me out healed and whole. Now I can help so many people through my experience have the same freedom I have.

You have to learn to take authority over your life and mind. It is easy to speak revenge but, why risk your purpose for the sake of getting even? Stop trying to retaliate against the people who have miss treated you. I can remember when the Lord spoke to me saying, "Joanna live in such a way when people see you they see a totally new person, live in such a way that when the people from your past speak evil about you it falls to their feet." I have not arrived, I am still a work in progress. That is why I can relate to you, your challenges, and your pain.

I know you too can be changed, healed, and made whole. Our lives affect others and it is important not to cause others pain. My divorce injured me but it also affected my daughters. They needed their momma to heal. After the divorce was final I moved in with my grandfather and grieved about everything I had lost. Everything was about me. I could not get past the reality of being an adult and mother yet I was becoming dependent on my widowed grandfather.

The rebellious independent girl who left home 10 years prior was far from independent anymore. I was back in my grandfathers home with my two girls who were confused, broken, and filled with anger and sadness. They did not deserve the humiliation of their mother having to start over. I knew I needed to be the mother they needed, but at the beginning of my healing process I did not know how to be anything other than depressed, sad, and angry. Besides my girls needing me healed, I needed myself healed.

For years I continued to mess up and not do the right things. My heart was still broken and I had always been able to fix my problems with temporary solutions however, none of that worked anymore. I had to face my problems head on and the reality of my life and it's imperfections overwhelmed me. I saw myself for everything I was not and everything I did not want to be. Such as a messed up divorced mother of two girls.

But God.. GOD helped me to restart my thinking process and see myself the way He saw me, as a woman He created in His image and likeness. I would call myself pitiful and He would call me powerful. I made the decision that I would cause no one pain anymore.

As you start forgiving yourself and receive Gods forgiveness, understand you will fall sometimes but, God never quits loving you, He never gives up on you.

Think about the Samaritan woman in John 4. She moved forward and allowed God to change her. In a moment God can change your entire life, even when everything in you wants to hide, get up and walk into victory. The enemy will keep sending distractions to prevent the person you will become on the other side of your trouble. Just fix your eyes on Jesus, on the breakthrough. You are not there yet but in Jesus name you will be soon.

The Bible says "Gods Word is lamp to our feet and a light to our path." see Psalms 119:105.

You must do your part, you must step out in faith. Fear is a spirit sent from the devil himself to paralyze you. I battled fear for the majority of my life, fear of tomorrow, fear of the unknown, fear of being alone, fear, fear, fear. It took me until I was thirty one years old to release that spirit I had held so close for all those years of my life. Honestly it took me so long to release it because before that I had never hit rock bottom and needed God so desperately as I did in that season of my life. There was no longer any way around it I had to take responsibility in my mess and stop blaming everyone else. I used to remind God as if He didn't already know how bad people were to me and every time I did all He would do is point out my need to heal. I finally broke down and surrendered to God and let Jesus take over and come into my heart.

I thought I had already done that at age fourteen but, if I had I would have never been filled with as much hatred as I had been fifteen years later. Like never before I started communicating with God praying His Will not mine. When God set me totally free it was as though I became a brand new person. My anger left, my brokenness left, I was healed like a puzzle shifted back together, back to how I was made to be. I became a woman on a mission opening my mouth declaring new things over myself. I allowed God to transform me into what He desired me to be. As you move forward on this journey to freedom release everything you've allowed to keep you in bondage. Invite Jesus into your life as your savior. He is ready and willing to do His part opening doors no man can shut.

I can not stress to you enough how important it is to keep your thoughts right. You do not have to think on every thought that comes into your mind. I used to act on pretty much every thought I had until I learned how to take my mind captive and only allow the Holy Spirit to speak. When I first started speaking out on spiritual topics self defeat would consume me. Who do you think you are? You never went to college, you are not educated enough to speak on this. People are going to judge you and criticize you for your past if you share it! You don't have all the answers, and then I remembered I am not the one doing this God is. He has educated me in the college of life and His Word.

Everyday I still have to renew my mind, be in the presence of the Lord, and continually prepare myself for the Holy Spirit to use me. Negative thinking holds us back from our freedom in

Christ Jesus. Life gets a whole lot easier when we stop living by others expectations and just do what we know God expects us to do. Which is let Him work through you. I love ministering to broken people, showing them the love God has for them, and helping them break free from bondage. I was chosen by God to do this!

CHAPTER FOUR

"For I know the plans I have for you; declares the Lord, plans to prosper you and not to harm you, plans to give you hope and a future." - Jeremiah 29:11

Because of our past we often allow the enemy to tell us we will never have what God has promised. Bondage is a real thing and it controls your mind.

You will never experience the salvation that Jesus died to give you if you allow your mind to stay captive with mistakes and people.

When doubt seeps into my mind God is quick to remind me He is well pleased with me and my actions. If I choose not to listen to God my thoughts would dictate my actions and more than likely grieve the Holy Spirit. You become what you think.

Paul wrote Philippians 4:6-8 in jail to teach us to stay peaceful in our thoughts. Fix your thoughts on what is true, noble, right, pure, lovely, admirable, excellent, and praiseworthy. Sometimes our circumstances can be quite opposite of peaceful. Thank you Jesus our peace does not come from circumstances. Here on earth we will never be free from opposition. Paul tells us nothing should worry us. We do not have to allow our conversations with people or stress to depict our peace. Changing our thoughts, changes our environments, and changes relationships.

You can be free from anxiety! How, because you have the mind of Christ! When you have the mind of Christ you can face difficulty without battling negative thoughts. Get in the Word of God, read your Bible, let it get into your heart and mind. There are some questions google can not answer. When worry seeps in remember prayer changes everything. In the middle of your mess focus on what is true, honorable, right, pure, lovely and admirable like Philippians 4:8, this will help you have the mind of Christ. Hearing about peace is one thing but when you obey Gods Word and experience it, it's another. Pray about everything and build up your faith. Pray expectantly knowing that every good and perfect gift comes from God.

I am not called to be perfect but I am called to be a vessel for God to use. Despite all of my imperfections God will shine brighter through me than I ever could in my own glory. We shut the devil up when we listen to and obey God. Those inner voices of doubt will keep us down as long as we let them. Matthew 5:45 The rain falls on the just and unjust. No one is immune to depression, we all experience something in life that would drive us towards it. But you have a choice to reject that outcome. Paul tells us in Philippians 4 it is possible, there is always a reason for every season and you can decide your pain will not be wasted and when you do that, the victory is yours!

Yes all those inner voices might be trying to drive you to destruction but you are the one in control of how you respond. Do not be fearful of your life or of the out outcome.

God has promised to work all things together for your good.

We often look at the situation we are in and think we are unwanted and rejected. But try to think of it this way, sometimes, rejection is Gods protection. satans mission is clear he can not hurt God so he hurts Gods people instead. You do not have to be a victim. You can pray your way out of anything you face. You must grasp exactly who you are in Christ and follow the example Jesus left for us. Even Jesus took time everyday to go to the Father in prayer. He understood He must be fueled by the power of God. If Jesus had to pull away from people and places to pray. How much more do we need to? Prayer is the path to freedom. Psalm 90:14 tells us to rejoice and be glad in our days. In times of trouble rejoice! If the devil did not see gifts and purpose in your future he would leave you alone. So pray your way through and watch how God shows up in your life.

After my divorce and returning to my grandparents home I could have stayed broken. Changing my life was my decision and if I would have figured that out sooner I would have saved myself a lot of stupid mistakes. Everyday I see people depressed and hurting wondering why God has not changed their situations. What they do not understand is it is their choice to make. None of us will know the things God has in store for us until we take a step towards Him. You can trust God, He has equipped you to come out of your current situation into a positive one but, it is up to you. I learned during that season of my life that God is good all the time, despite the outcome. I now look back on my past and realize that it was God who got me out of all those difficult situations and His Grace has kept me alive. He taught me how to break through the feeling of being overcome with sadness and how to replace those feelings with worship and His Word.

At times I have experienced a mental oppression that was almost physical, bringing heaviness and self defeating thoughts. I have come to realize at those times I am in the midst of a spiritual war and the only way to free myself is to pray and read Gods Word. Reading Ephesians 6 has helped me at these times and worship. There is not one person living today that should not be worshipping God. Worship changes things, it changes us, it changes the way we see God and ourselves. No matter how insecure, bitter, angry, or unhappy you are when you start to sing praises to God something shifts on the inside of you. Chains start breaking and falling. I had struggled with depression, hopelessness, and shame but, when I learned how to purse God. I discovered what freedom truly looks like.

First Peter 5:7-9 says: "Cast all your anxiety [cares] on him because he cares for you. Be alert and of sober mind. Your enemy the devil prowls around like a roaring lion looking for someone to devour. Resist him, standing firm in the faith."

I have learned that the way to resist the enemy, (the fool that got himself kicked out of Heaven and keeps trying to take your life into a downward spiral), is by casting your cares on the One who truly cares for you, Your Heavenly Father.

When my mind becomes filled with troubles the way I renew it is to listen to praise and worship music and sing along even when I don't feel like it. It shifts my focus from my problem to the power I have over that problem. The Spirit of God in you is greater than the challenges before you. This is when peace comes, not because my thoughts are right but because my heart is. Only Jesus Christ can defeat the enemy so when you see the devil at work in your life call on Jesus.

Fight with prayer, scripture, and worship.

Even when you are aware of Gods goodness and love, you will

still have to choose your thoughts. When Paul told us to only think about things that are pure and holy he was telling us we must decide how to think. When my mind starts to race I have to consciously think about what Im thinking about and if it does not align with Gods Word I kick it to the curb. To know if it aligns you have to feed on the word of God.

You are in a battle for your mind and you need to decide you are a warrior and you will be victorious!

CHAPTER FIVE

Rejection is painful and we will all experience the feeling of rejection at some point in our lives. Rejection is often the root cause of bitterness, un-forgiveness, and pain. However it does not have to be that way. Rejection is not always a bad thing. If you are rejected by a person or job accept that it was not Gods plan for you. Rejection can be a blessing in disguise, it can be God's protection. Fear of being rejected is a deep-rooted fear that affects many. When we live afraid that someone might disapprove of or reject us, this fear seeps into the very pores of who we are. We hesitate to trust others or engage in relationships because we doubt we will be accepted. Past hurts keep many of us from opening up and living in freedom. Rather than dealing with the pain of the past and moving on in God, we rehearse the pain and live captive to a fear that it will happen again.

Rejection that can drain you and get you stuck is the rejection of a father abandoning you or a spouse leaving you. This rejection can be so painful it can alter the way you see the world. It is very possible to overcome this pain and walk in Gods fullness despite others failures. The Bible gives great hope to the person who has been rejected and unwanted: Jesus understands the pain because He experienced it Himself. He understands the feelings that come when people push you away and make you feel devalued. Perhaps that is why Jesus used the final verse in the book of Matthew to tell His disciples:... And behold, I am with you all the days (perpetually, uniformly, and on every occasion), to the (very) close and consummation of the age. Even in His final moments on earth Jesus wanted them to know they are never alone. Though others might reject and abandon them, He never would.

I am no stranger to rejection. My biological father chose drugs and alcohol over me and my siblings. As a little girl I was crushed and was not able to wrap my head around why my daddy did not want me, as an adult now I see Gods protection.

If my biological father would have stayed in our lives he would have done more damage than good. There is no perfect person, no perfect relationship, no perfect marriage. Even with the best of intentions people will fail us time to time. Through a lifetime of pain I have learned no matter how perfectly your relationship starts out, you can not be good enough, pretty enough, or skilled enough to maintain perfect harmony all the time. You and your spouse have many faults and failures and if you do not set things right daily you will be asking yourself why did it have to end this way.

Bad things happen in life even to good people. I missed out on my own childhood, being the eldest I was left home to care for my younger siblings while my mother chose friends and drugs over her family. I felt betrayed and rejected because I never had the security I needed to enjoy being young. Life deals many hard blows and no one comes out untouched. The pain you feel might not be from something you have done, life can just be unfair. People sometimes blame God for their pain wondering why He allowed it.

Let me tell you God never ever puts pain and suffering on anyone. However He is always there during this those hard times. He said He would never leave us nor forsake us. Family and home should be a safe place but too often it is full of abuse, betrayal, and molestation. When a child is molested it begins a long trail of seeking love in all the wrong places. You might be that child, your son or daughter might be that child.

Others sin has affected you, you were betrayed by those you thought would protect you. However giving yourself away to person after person will only set you up for more harm than you ever imagined. Your answer is found at the cross. Think on this as well, real men lead women to Jesus, not to their bedrooms!

You may not be responsible for your wound but you are most definitely responsible for your healing! One of the greatest damages from rejection is the self inflicted pain it brings.

You may feel worthless but, God has never made anything that was not of a great worth! You hear God made us each special but you live with the fear of rejection and harden your heart to cover your hurt.

God never leaves us in our pain and rejection. He deliberately sets divine appointments for you to meet people who say the right thing at the right time to pull you out of your pit. Watch for those words of encouragement, words of knowledge, generous acts, and Jesus loves you, they are all from heaven!

Some decisions can bring a hell on earth situation but God says we are fearfully and wonderfully made. Gods thoughts towards us are immeasurably good. We will never be able to count them. When you realize God loves you beyond your ability to ever love, it breaks the fear of rejection and the feeling of being unloved. You are not what people have called you. You are not how you feel about yourself. You are who God says you are. You are fearfully and wonderfully made. Your strength is in God and realizing this will break the bondage you are living in.

You can become an unstoppable force living in this world. You do not have to live in your brokenness, you can leave it behind. How? Jesus! You have a Savior that went to the cross at Calvary to take your sins and suffering in His body. He did it so you can become righteous and set free.

We can not change people and we do not have to continue to subject ourselves to people who reject and humiliate us. Love them from a far. We will all experience rejection but it is our responsibility to handle it in a Godly manner and move on.

The grace of God is the only reason I have been able to move on and walk in forgiveness. I had to learn to forgive continually to finally break free from the pain. Memories of my pain and rejection always seemed to try to resurface. I had to learn to be stronger than my struggles and speak life back into myself. I have never met a strong person that had an easy past. Speaking life over yourself will create a strong character. Your character is more important than your reputation.

Jesus had to lose His reputation to do the will of God, but His character today is excellent all around the world. Your character is who you really are, your reputation is who people think you are. I now refuse to allow anyone who is not in my life have any say in what they think or feel about me. Whenever negative thoughts try to creep in I quickly center myself back to what God has done in me, for me, and through me. I speak life. I am redeemed, not rejected! You too can break free from those painful memories, replace them with good thoughts, good people, and people that bring you closer to Jesus. I can not change my past but I can and will have a great future.

Grab hold of the power God has given you, move on and become the person God created you to be.

We make excuses for everything, blame others and never take responsibility for our own actions. We might get knocked down sometimes but, we are not knocked out! I once lived a life controlled by my excuses. As a child I accepted the labels family, friends, peers, and teachers put on me. I accepted them as though I was really those names. I allowed what they said to dictate how I functioned. I allowed what they said to be what I saw in the mirror.

It took me close to thirty years to understand that I am not what others say I am and that I can change. That I could forgive those who overlooked me and those who labeled me. That I did not have to live with a victim mentality just because peoples words and actions had injured me. Forgiveness was the key to moving past hurts. Just because you talk to someone and are friendly does not mean your heart has truly forgiven them. How we deal with a situation has a lot to do with how that situation will turn out.

When we face difficult challenges in life we often lose sight of our blessings. We sometimes lose sight of what God has already brought us out of. When I look back at my life I can see now where God met me in the middle of my storms and redeemed me from a path of failure. I never expected to overcome the consequences of my poor decisions.

We can pick our sin but, most definitely can not pick our consequences! I used to think this is as good as it gets, I am stuck living in drama, not just my own but, others drama as well. God is so good to us even though we do not deserve it.

When I stood there facing the consequences of all that I had allowed in my life, the choice was clear to receive the peace and unconditional love I had never known. I would have to change my actions. You reap what you sow and I was definitely reaping.

I had spent years judging how others lived and blaming them for my pain. I often thought why was my ex so perfect in my eyes until we got married. Why had he not become what I dreamed, the protector I desperately needed. I finally realized I was part of that problem and quit blaming him.

Never try to destroy someone's life with a lie, when yours can be destroyed with the truth.

Making excuses for my anger was not helping my girls who were just as heartbroken as I was. Because they as well had also lost everything they had known. I could not keep blaming my ex I had to step up and be accountable for my own actions and misjudgments. As much as I suffered, my girls suffered too.

I knew I had to quit blaming and start forgiving if anything was ever going to change and if I ever expected my girls to do the same.

As we grow up we become what we see being modeled before us. If your home is peaceful your children will feel secure and loved but, if your home is full of turmoil and strife they will develop feelings of distrust and loneliness which will ultimately lead to anxiety and depression and behavioral issues. For years I used my stressful and turmoil filled childhood as an excuse to make mistakes. In order to grow and live the abundant life we are all called to live we have to first learn to forgive! Over the years I have let myself run out of excuses and forgive all the hurt. I no longer blame the bad choices I have made on others.

We can not control everything that takes place in our lives it is only when we allow God to work in us that change can come. I used to love to diagnose myself with obsessive compulsive disorder also known as OCD and always try to micromanage everything.

It was not until God showed me that when I always tried to control everything, down to which way a picture was turned it put me in strife with those around me. So often we have expectations of the way things "should be" it leads us to make bad decisions that ultimately affect those around us. I had such high expectations and could never understand why not one person could meet them. I lived constantly disappointed. Unwillingly, I had finally come to the point it was time to reap the consequences of every action I had ever taken. My time of running away from my issues was up and I hit rock bottom, hard. Let me tell you there is only one good thing about losing everything and hitting your head at rock bottom. It is finding out who that rock is, and His name is Jesus Christ.

That rock I hit so hard is what my entire redemption story is based upon. Jesus turned me right side up and propelled me right out of that pit! That is one of the amazing things about God, when we surrender to Him, He says your time of pain, suffering, and heartache is up, and it is time for a fresh start child.

When God is ready to propel you into your destiny not one of those excuses you have used in the past or the ill words others say and think of you, will persuade Him to do otherwise. You will never change Gods mind about you or the plan He has for you. God works with each of us right where we are and He determines where we will go. God has called each of us to be great, to live lives of excellence. I believe when we become honest with ourselves about our shortcomings we free ourselves to be used by God. When God calls you out of your situation trust that you can find rest in Him.

After a failed marriage you may convince yourself you just need to be alone or that you need to experience things you think being married kept you back from. No, no, and no. These paths lead to destruction. You will find yourself in even more difficult situations that ultimately lead to soul ties. If you think celibacy is hard, try breaking a soul tie! A soul tie can serve many functions, but in its simplest form, it ties two souls together in the spiritual realm. Unholy soul ties can be used as bridges to pass demonic garbage between two people. The devil uses soul ties to his advantage to fill your spirit with every unholy, unclean thing he can.

Have you ever found yourself tormented by thoughts about a person, excessively wondering about them, checking on them, and rehearsing times with them? If so, you have soul ties. Soul ties are formed through close friendships, through vows, commitments and promises, and through physical intimacy. The Bible gives us many accounts of both good and bad soul ties. Some examples are...

"After David had finished talking with Saul, he met Jonathan, the king's son. There was an immediate bond between them, for Jonathan loved David." 1 Samuel 18:1

"My child, if sinners entice you, turn your back on them." Proverbs 1:10

"My child, don't go along with them! Stay far away from their paths." Proverbs 1:15

"And don't you realize that if a man joins himself to a prostitute, he becomes one body with her?

For the Scriptures say, "The two are united into one." 1 Corinthians 6:16

"But if we confess our sins to him, he is faithful and just to forgive us our sins and to cleanse us from all wickedness." 1 John 1:9

You can never fall so far from God that you can not be

restored. He is an "I do not care how far you have run, just come home" kind of God. Repenting and accepting His forgiveness restores the standard in your life, and you can live in freedom and hope again.

Get honest with yourself. You either suffer the pain of discipline or you will suffer the pain of regret. The only way to be free from fear is to stop allowing it to control how you are going to live.

Do not be so afraid to wait for the right Godly man or right Godly woman that you get yourself into a mess that took you one night to get into and will take you years to get out of. Sexually transmitted demons are no respecters of condoms, do not be fooled! Be intentional about your future. We do not get do overs, your past will always be your past but, thank you Jesus we get a fresh tomorrow to not make the same mistakes.

Roman 12:2 says "not to be conformed to this world but be transformed by the renewing of your mind." In the fallen world we live in today no one can claim to never disappoint or hurt anyone. The only way to live holy the way the Bible tells us to is to be transformed by Jesus Christ, accept Him as Lord of your life, and allow Him to renew your mind and transform you day by day. Accept that you have made mistakes and have fallen short in the past and get on with your life. Making excuses only creates more self- centeredness. If you can not allow others to speak into your life without getting upset with them, it is time to admit you have an issue that is preventing your growth.

Durning my years of healing I realized growth just does not happen. I was set free and healed but did not grow until I took the first steps. I started feeding on Gods Word, watching tv sermons, and reading. Then within what felt like a short period of time a fire was sparked inside me for more. I started spending more time hearing and talking about Jesus than I did talking to, or about other people. I have grown at such a rapid rate that if you knew me six months ago its probably a good idea for me to introduce myself again.

This growth was the result of persistently seeking God and understanding His plan. Often the gap of who we are and what we can be is filled with disbelief and habits. We begin to believe everything people say even when we know it is not true. Some people in life will build you up, telling you how great you are when you know you could do so much better but, that is where we get stuck, we accept the unacceptable. These people who never encourage you to do better than you have in the past are not your real friends.

At some point in life, every person must decide whether they will be a "people-pleaser" or a "God-pleaser." Our goal should be to please God no matter what the cost. Real friends are honest, they will tell you when you need to change and they will love you along the way. When you are a good person you do not lose friends, they lose you. You need people in your life who you can trust and that will be honest with you especially through your rougher seasons. Not just telling you what you want to hear. Allow wisdom from others to be spoken into your situations. Do not allow someone with a messy life tell you how to live yours. Find a friend who has walked through a hell on earth situation but is now healed and is walking in the plan God has for them. That friend will be filled with wisdom and knowledge. You also need people who will allow you to be honest with them throughout their seasons as well. Friendship is not a one way street. I have had many different types of friends in all different seasons and I have learned the hard way that if they are not allowing you to pour into them as much as they pour into you or vise versa it is not a true friendship. Give as much as you take.

Jesus tells us in Matthew 16:24 to "deny ourselves, take up our cross and follow Him."

When we deny ourselves we can focus on God. Not everything is about us! Even what others think or say about us, is not about us. Why let people and situations determine our attitude? Why are you giving a person so much power over yourself? Do not rob yourself of joy because someone does not agree with you. The same Spirit that rose Jesus from the grave lives on the inside of you. We have the power to let go of ourselves and make decisions that will bring glory to God but, you have to make that choice. Many substance abusers use their upbringing to make excuses for their failures. My father was an alcoholic or my mother was a drug addict are common excuses for why they live as they do and can not break their habit. They convince themselves that there is no use in trying to be better.

I was the first person in my family for generations and generations back to sell out to the Lord. My mothers side of the family were all born and raised into the Jehovah Witnesses and my fathers side did not really believe there was even a God.

But as you can tell I am not an example follower, I am a generational curse breaker! My grandmother who was raised a Jehovah Witness made the decision to send me to a tongue speaking, spirit filled private school. It was a culture shock to me to say the least but, that one decision set a foundation for me that years later I am firmly standing upon. It was not until after my divorce I had realized, I had taken on many of my family's generational patterns. For so many years I had vowed that I would never be like my mother or father in certain areas of my life, yet as an adult, I found myself doing the exact things I loathed.

Did you grow up in a home in which your mother would scream? Or with a father who had a problem with anger? Have you vowed, I will never act like my mother or father and yet chances are today you have done exactly what you did not want to do. Maybe you suffer from anxiety and fear or depression and you have come to realize your parents and grandparents did as well. People say "Like father, like son." Just as this is true in genetics, it is also true in the spiritual realm of our family.

Some examples of generational curses can be family illnesses that are passed down from one person to the next. Anxiety, alcoholism, eating disorders, sexual abuse, physical abuse, manipulation and control, constant financial difficulties, mental problems, addiction, adultery, and the list can go on.

Anything that seems to be a persistent struggle or problem passed down from one generation to another may very well be a generational curse. Just as we inherited the curse of sin from Adam and Eve through generations, we also inherit the tendency to sin the same way our ancestors have.

You need to understand there is a cycle that needs to be broken. You are not supposed to suffer through life with destructive behavior and simply accept it because it is viewed as family history.

Some patterns you may view as normal is because you have

never known anything different. The cycle can be broken! My past and my family history was a lesson to be learned. Because I refuse to have a dysfunctional household and family, my children will serve the Lord and walk out the divine calling God has on their lives in peace and fully loved. I stopped making excuses and chose to change.

Declare that healing runs in your family!

Because of my heritage I never knew the power in Gods Word and the power that Jesus died to give me. I am able to see now that my parents were simply replicating the patterns they had seen and experienced growing up.

My mom had more bad days then good, and it was a rare thing to hear my mother say the words I love you while I was growing up. Her love was conditional and depended upon her mood for that day and what was done for her. She at times could be kind but, more often, she would be very cruel with her words and actions. I used to think it was my fault when my mother was upset but, now I can see the pain of generational anger and hurt that my mother carried was very deep. It is important to understand that things do not ever just work themselves out. Everything must be intentional.

The issues of the past need to be confronted and dealt with. We are all broken in some way, and the only way to find true freedom is to go directly to the One who made us and knows our past better than we do. God is the only one with the power to work all things together for our good. Your cycle of brokenness can stop if you allow God to heal your hurts and break the strongholds.

In my past, I have witnessed damage done in my siblings and extended family members due to abuse and anger. This reinforced how truly broken our family was and how behaviors are so ingrained in our thinking and living, I had believed there was no way out. I had believed these things were out of my control, and that what was done to me, and spoken over me had hardened my heart forever.

Transformation is not impossible. There is a hope.

Jesus came to bring freedom to the oppressed and healing to all who will receive it. The enemy wants us to believe the lie that we can never be healed from the pain and damage done to us.

There is no pain, no sin, no damage that God cannot heal! He heals the brokenhearted.

As a young adult I had gained the mentality of "it is what it is" and "if ya can't beat them, join them." I believed satan's lies and I learned to cope. I have come to realize that through encountering God, when Jesus died on the cross, He took every curse and iniquity upon His shoulders and declared "It is finished." Strongholds will not go away by themselves. Only when we allow God to take over we find freedom.

Ask Jesus to reveal to you the strongholds that are stopping you from living in the fullness of freedom. Replace all the lies the devil has told you with the truth. The process of healing my wounds in my heart did not happen overnight. I had to learn to wait on God and get to know Him personally. Over time, I allowed Him to speak into my heart and replace the lies with His truth. Do not phone a friend every time something happens in your life, take time and talk to God about it. No one can change a situation for you. You must chose and commit to change. I lived in the valley for almost thirty years until I made the choice. I was so tired of making excuses and thinking strife and turmoil was the normal. If I would have known how God was going to heal me, mold me, and use me I would have let Him a lot sooner than I did. You can go from making excuses because it runs in the family, to change making. It may have run in my family but, this is where it runs out! Forgive those who have caused you pain and suffering. Forgive your parents who where absent when you needed them. Forgive the friend who betrayed you and forgive the family member who molested you. Do not hold onto the pain, you will only hurt yourself.

Repeat Philippians 4:13 over yourself daily "I can do all things through Christ who gives me strength."

If you let go of the pain you will find the solid ground in which true healing and heart transformation can take place. You can not afford to keep harboring hurt and making excuses. Forgive others as your Heavenly Father has forgiven you.

CHAPTER SIX

So many times we make a choice to change and yet go right back to our old ways the second a conflict arrises. I was up and down every other day for years wanting change. Sometimes difficult seasons are necessary for God to draw out what He wants from us. I had allowed the enemy to steal my joy for years but, after my breakthrough, I also allowed God to pick me up, mold me, and use me as His vessel.

Today what you see in public is the result of what took place in private.

For years, a tug of war took place in my heart and mind. I nearly gave into Satan's lies, believing I was worthless but, then I met Jesus. I was attending a revival in Arkansas several years ago, where I was called out to from the crowd by the gentleman leading it. He said daughter, God is going to return everything the devil has stolen from you. My heart sank! I didn't know this man, how did he know I had things stolen, no one there knew anything about my past. As he prayed over me I fell under the spirit.

The presence of God around me, His Holiness was too powerful for me to fight. I could hear everyone standing over me praying. And I had heard the voice of God whisper Joanna it is time, I am healing you please stop fighting me. God was putting me back together. I allowed Him to come into all of my broken places and fix my broken pieces. I could feel the heartache leaving my chest and God's peace and love flowing back in.

His love overwhelmed me!

When I finally got to my feet I felt so full like all the pain, and strife, and heartache that was on my heart was gone and it was now full of peace, and a love I had never felt before.

That day I was handed a piece of paper and written on it was Philippians 4:6 "Do not be anxious or worried about anything, but in everything by prayer and petition with thanksgiving, continue to make your requests known to God."

I still to this day have that piece of paper stuck in my Bible.

Jesus will fix all of your broken pieces and hold your hand through the process. He will kindly and patiently walk with you. "As you draw close to Him, He will draw close to you." - James 4:8

I discovered that I am a daughter of a King. That I was predestined before the foundation of the world to do good works, which He prepared in advance for me to do (Ephesians 2:10).

He transformed my brokenness so that the world can see how He truly gives beauty for ashes (Isaiah 61:3).

He turned my sorrow into joy (Jeremiah 31:13).

He gave me the tools to help me forgive my ex husband, my mother, my father, and anyone else who had hurt me. God intends for our lives to inspire others. The label I chose to were is His, I am a daughter of the Most High God, Capable, Worthy, Chosen, Known, Loved, Redeemed, and Accepted.

You have to learn you have to cooperate with what God wants to do in your life. You have to start adding action to your prayers and do whatever it takes to move out of undesirable situations and have a want to be made whole. Shake off complacency and fully grasp that when you decide its time for a change, change will come!

If I would have just waited for others to change or a situation to change I would still be stuck, filled with anger and left feeling rejected. Promotion comes from God, not the people you surround yourself with. Most of the time the people around you truly do not want you to go to the next level. Growth takes time and choices must be made for change to happen.

You have to chose to believe, Jesus is a gentleman and He will not just command you to do something, He simply asks and we only need obey.

Being a Christian does not mean that you will automatically be free from pain of memories. In Christ our thoughts become brand new. We quit defending when we surrender. To become new you must purse a personal relationship with Him. As you seek God and surrender to Him, you let go of your own ways and mindsets and start to see from God's point of view. This creates in you the mind of Christ. You cannot make anyone change. You can, however, Change will not come suddenly because, you did not get to how you are today, overnight. Looking back before my divorce I was simply not mature in Christ on any level. I did not know how to pray let alone have patience. Becoming a mature believer means understanding God's position in your life, He is our Father. Many Bible stories are about people who struggled for years yet, stayed in faith believing that God would see them through. When I was younger I used to think I have so much time to accomplish everything I want to do. I wasted twenty plus years of my life thinking I had plenty of time. When reality finally hit, my girls were broken and our family was filled with strife and turmoil.

I am so thankful God gave me another chance to make the right decisions and break free from selfishness. Life is much shorter than I had once thought but, God graciously gave me time to set things right. He has taken everything that had broken me and used it to restore me. I can not begin to describe the loneliness I felt as I walked through my healing journey with no one but Jesus.

I had to let go of everyone who assisted in creating chaos in my life. I had to stop the roller coaster ride and learn to sit while allowing God to root out all the negatives that had become my way of life. You will never be content taking depression medications and sleeping pills. Contentment always comes at a price, we have to come to the end of ourselves and realize that things around us cannot make us happy. We need to learn to stop comparing our lives to others. The society we live in today sets false values on absolutely everything. The next best thing on the market will not help you in your darkest hour!

What if instead of restoring just what was lost, God wanted to give you something you have never had before? Double for your trouble!

One of my favorite verses says, "Behold, I will do a new thing, now it shall spring forth; shall you not know it? I will even make a road in the wilderness and rivers in the desert" - Isaiah 43:19.

No matter how broken you feel today, God can bring you to the path He made long before you were born. You may be tired, discouraged, and frustrated, but do not give up. Your situation will change! When we develop a habit of praying instead of being anxious or complaining, your attitude toward everything will change. Expectation is the strong belief that something will happen.

Expectation is also actively standing on faith.

Through my healing I began to believe God will not only restore all that I had lost but also give me restitution for all that the enemy had stolen from me. Double for my trouble! Sometimes you must change for your situation around you to change. Let go of negative thoughts. We as christians are to go one way that is from glory to glory. The glory is great but no one ever talks about the "to" (the valley). We all want to see change in some area of our lives but we need direction and guidance. The “to” is what we have to walk through to get to the great God has for us.

The lesson I have learned is that God is always working on our behalf, even when we fail to see it. He has a perfect plan, and His timing is perfect.

“Our steps are always ordered by the Lord” (Psalm 37:23).

“We cannot lean on our own understanding because it is limited” (Proverbs 3:5).

“The Lord opens doors that no one can shut and that no one else could open” (Revelation 3:7).

Do not despise the valley. Eventually the valley season comes to an end. It is during the “to” the valley season that the Lord is setting you up for the glory that is to come. I used to resent where I came from and the cards that life had dealt me. I often spent my days wishing for someone else's life, wishing I looked different, wishing I had the talents others where celebrated for. I looked at what I did not have instead of what I did have.

I desperately wanted to feel I was accepted and that I belonged, but instead I found myself feeling ordinary and unworthy.

It took me many years before I understood that my life was in Gods hands and He had a unique purpose for me. He would turn my mess into a message, my test into a testimony, and my faults into fruits that others could taste and see the goodness of Jesus. I learned that my life experiences, whether good or bad, seasons of plenty or lack, would set me on a course of discovering what

I was made of and who I belonged to.

God would direct me to others like me, to help me bring breakthrough to them, the people others found hard to relate to. My weaknesses in His power would become strengths, and every negative situation would be turned into a positive.

I began to see that the negative things that happened in my life, which were meant to destroy me, actually became the part of me that can help other people find freedom. Instead of looking at how imperfect my parents were, I now see the positive that I was blessed with an amazing grandmother that took me in when I felt so unloved and she repositioned my sails right towards God.

CHAPTER SEVEN

Since I was a child my deepest longing was to help people. I believe that is because I longed to be helped so much. I come alive when talking to people and helping them through their own struggles. I had always felt I could help people from despair. Little did I know God had placed in my heart purpose for a life healing ministry.

Because of my experiences, I can empathize with people who have gone through similar situations and give them the keys to finding freedom. It took me a long time but, my life now makes sense and I understand my purpose. God turned around what the enemy meant for evil, and He made it beautiful.

Being vulnerable no longer brought me shame; instead, my honesty enabled others to feel safe and break free. They could say, "If she can do it, then so can I." Out of obedience to God my life began to inspire others and that caused me to thrive.

I truly believe we are meant to inspire others to freedom, to help them discover who they are in Christ. We should always imitate the characteristics of Jesus and God gives us grace to enable us to live according to His plan and purpose.

The secret to finding your true identity is not a diet plan or a quick fix pill. It is simply a life surrendered to Jesus. Day by day you may not notice the change, but after a while, you will look back and see how far you have grown. For years, a tug-of-war took place in my heart and mind. I nearly gave into satan's lies, believing I was insignificant and worthless. One day I met Jesus, and I allowed Him to come into those broken places and hold my hand through the process and show me what it truly meant when He said, "I have come that they may have life, and have it to the full" (John 10:10).

When I handed over control to Him and gave Him my life, I did as He asked. Jesus walked patiently with me. He began to shred the hurt and hardened layers off of my heart.

"And as I drew close to Him, He drew close to me" (James 4:8).

"He has never left me or forsaken me" (Hebrews 13:5).

"He turned my sorrow into joy" (Jeremiah 31:13).

If I had continued to listen to satan's lies, I would have never overcome a failed marriage, disappointing my daughters, and all my self destruction. Because of Gods Grace I continue to marvel at how beautiful my life is. The world needs to see the transformation that took place on the inside of you. I pray this book has helped you understand that no matter what your past looks like, you are God's child and He has not given up on you.

"Beloved, I pray that you may prosper in all things and be in health, just as your soul prospers." (3 John 2).

Because of my experiences with pain and rejection, it is easy for me to recognize both in the faces I encounter daily. I survived my past in order to help others survive theirs. The truth is we serve a good father who wants us whole and healed. The God I love and serve does not want any of His children brokenhearted.

In my life I have come to realize hurt people hurt people and healed people heal people. I am on a journey that will continue on until the day I stand before God and He says "Well done, good and faithful servant" (Matthew 25:21).

It is important for you to believe in God and believe that He will see you through your darkest times. Your pain is real, but you can be free. Throughout this book I am offering you the most real solution to your problems money can not buy: Jesus

Christ. I testify of God's goodness in my life to give you hope in your hopeless situation. Just as God has a plan for your life, Satan has a plot to steal, kill, and destroy you.

Perseverance is the key to breakthrough.

Scripture tells us, "Do not cast away your confidence, which has great reward. For you have need of endurance, so that you have done the will of God, you may receive the promise" - Hebrews 10:35-36.

We sometimes tend to stop short of what God has promised us. We give up right before our breakthrough. We allow fear to seep in and we lose sight of our purpose. Set your mind to persevere until you see the promises of God in your life.

Get so busy living a new life that you will never allow anyone to pull you back into your old one.

"All the promises of God in Him are yes, and in Him Amen, to the glory of God through us" (2 Corinthians 1:20). Make up your mind that no matter how difficult life is you will never give up!

Instead of telling God how big your mountain is, tell that mountain how big your God is. Remember David was never moved by the size of Goliath or the volume of his threats. He was moved by the size of his God and the power in His name. Only God can redeem all of your failures. God is concerned with what is taking place on the inside of you and healing takes time. I always say if it took you 10 years to get into that mess, it will take you ten years to get out and fully healed. Do not give up, you can do this. When it is seeming like you are taking one step forward and two steps back remember why the devil is fighting you and it will help you refocus and push forward.

When you choose to change and grow it is a process that takes place and is very uncomfortable at times. Your current situation is not a permanent destination. Expect change,

let your faith direct your life.

God is no respecter of persons, He wants to heal you and make you just as whole as He has me. Your number one priority must be making Jesus Lord of your life, there is no other way. Make spending more time with God a priority.

The world gave up on me, took everything from me and made

me start all over again. Even at times I thought God had left me, He was there working behind the scenes. He has shown me over and over how faithful He is. I trust Him that if I do my part, He will do His. He has shown me that even a pregnant high school drop out, divorced, continually making mistakes will have the greatest comeback story.

Looking back on my past while writing this book, I can say this: I would go back and do it all again but, I would not trade a tear. I would just wish I could get to this place I am now in life a little sooner. I have watched God restore my life. I have watched Him bring better people in and take some out. I can talk to my daughters about the past and instead of hurt and tears we have joy. They get to watch their mother love people, bring them into the kingdom of God, and help them heal from their pasts. I have been given the best husband in the world, who loves me and my daughters. He is very proud of the woman I have become.

We all live in peace.

Years ago I would have never dreamed my life would look the way it does. I am so thankful God never gave up on me, and He will never give up on you. I am thankful that I realized some people are only in our lives for a season.

Your healing is on the other side of letting go. I believe in you, you can do this. God never stops believing in you. You are bold and you are fearfully and wonderfully made. It is a new season! If Jesus is your Lord and Savior, you are the child of the most high God. God loves you more than you could ever know. As you have been reading this book I have been praying, that you clearly hear God's voice speaking to you.

I would like to ask you to sit for a moment close your eyes and ask God to direct you to verses in your Bible that speak His truth into your life. This will help you replace the lies you may have been speaking over yourself, with His truth.

No matter what your past looks like, remember you are loved and have a heavenly Father waiting with arms wide open for you to turn to Him. You are special and beautifully made. You are a survivor! You are a warrior and when people ask you how you have survived thus far remember to tell them, Jesus, it has always been Jesus.

ABOUT THE AUTHOR

Joanna Beck, is a kingdom minded disciple of Jesus Christ, Holy Spirit- filled daughter of God who is not afraid to speak bold and courageous Truth to a generation being crushed under the weight of their sins, circumstances, and lies of the enemy. She is a wife, mother, leader, and friend. Very passionate about encountering God and having a personal relationship with Jesus. Considers it a privilege to be pursuing the abundant life God has called her too. Since being redeemed she lives with the mission to decrease hells population. With this book Joanna hopes to encourage people to live in the fullness God has for them and equip them to rise up in the days we are living in, put the devil under their feet and be the warrior God has created them to be. She believes you are capable, you are worthy, you are valuable, you are chosen, you are known, you are redeemed, you are accepted, and you are so loved by your Heavenly Father!

Made in the USA
Columbia, SC
02 June 2019